I0796310

DISCOVERING THE UNITED STATES

Connecticut

BY IB LARSEN

An Imprint of Abdo Publishing
abdobooks.com

abdobooks.com

Published by Abdo Publishing, a division of ABDO, PO Box 398166, Minneapolis, Minnesota 55439.

Printed in China.
052024
092024

Cover Photo: Thomas Roche/Moment/Getty Images
Interior Photos: Randy Duchaine/Alamy, 4–5; Comet Design/Shutterstock Images, 7; Mira/Alamy, 8, 28 (bottom left); Jukka Jantunen/Shutterstock Images, 10 (top left); Shutterstock Images, 10 (top right), 24; Shutterstock Images, 10 (bottom left); iStockphoto, 10 (bottom right); Joseph Presiozo/AFP/Getty Images, 12–13; North Wind Picture Archives/Alamy, 15; Sean Elliot/NCAA Photos/Getty Images, 16; Mark Lennihan/AP Images, 18; Winston Tan/Shutterstock Images, 20–21, 28 (bottom right); Jan Gorzynik/Alamy, 22; James Kirkikis/Shutterstock Images, 26; Red Line Editorial, 28 (top), 29

Editor: Haley Williams
Series Designer: Katharine Hale

Library of Congress Control Number: 2023949338

Publisher's Cataloging-in-Publication Data

Names: Larsen, Ib, author.
Title: Connecticut / by Ib Larsen
Description: Minneapolis, Minnesota: Abdo Publishing, 2025 | Series: Discovering the United States | Includes online resources and index.
Identifiers: ISBN 9781098293772 (lib. bdg.) | ISBN 9798384913047 (ebook)
Subjects: LCSH: U.S. states--Juvenile literature. | Connecticut--History--Juvenile literature. | Northeastern States--Juvenile literature. | Physical geography--United States--Juvenile literature.
Classification: DDC 973--dc23

All population data taken from:
"Estimates of Population by Sex, Race, and Hispanic Origin: April 1, 2020 to July 1, 2022." *US Census Bureau, Population Division*, June 2023, census.gov.

CONTENTS

This model of the *Turtle* submarine at the Connecticut River Museum has a side removed so visitors can sit inside.

CHAPTER 1

The *Turtle* Submarine

It was the morning of September 7, 1776. A submarine was about to enter battle for the first time. American **colonists** were fighting for independence from Great Britain in the Revolutionary War (1775–1783).

American pilot Ezra Lee sneakily approached a British ship in the submarine. He planned to sink the ship with explosives. However, he couldn't properly attach the explosives to the ship. Lee had to give up. But then, British soldiers spotted him. Lee released the explosives behind him to scare away the soldiers. He returned to the shore unharmed.

The Provisions State

Connecticut was an important part of the Revolutionary War. It became known as the **Provisions** State. The state supplied much of the American army's food and equipment. The British attacked Connecticut several times to destroy supplies. But in the end, the Americans defeated the British and won the war.

The Connecticut state flag shows the Latin phrase *Qui Transtulit Sustinet.* It translates to "He who transplanted still sustains."

The submarine Lee was in was known as the *Turtle.* It was called that because it was shaped like a turtle shell. The *Turtle* was designed and built in the state of Connecticut.

Kent Falls State Park features one of many large waterfalls that feed into Connecticut's rivers.

Today, people can visit the Connecticut River Museum. It is located in Essex. They can see a life-size model of the *Turtle* submarine there.

Connecticut's Land

Connecticut is in the Northeast region of the United States. It was one of the 13 original British **colonies**. The state's neighbors were also original colonies. Connecticut is south of Massachusetts. Rhode Island is to the east, and New York is to the west. The state's southern coast is on the Atlantic Ocean.

Connecticut has forests, hills, and beaches. The eastern and western parts of the state are hilly. The central part is flat.

Connecticut Facts

DATE OF STATEHOOD
January 9, 1788

CAPITAL
Hartford

POPULATION
3,626,205

AREA
5,543 square miles
(14,356 sq km)

STATE BIRD

American robin

STATE TREE

Charter oak

STATE FLOWER

Mountain laurel

STATE SHELLFISH

Eastern oyster

Each US state has a different population, size, and capital city. States also have state symbols.

There are many lakes and rivers as well. Animals living in Connecticut include deer, wild turkeys, and American robins. The American robin is the state bird.

Connecticut's Climate

Connecticut has four seasons. In the winter, the state gets a lot of snow. The snow on the ground usually melts by March as temperatures rise.

Connecticut's summers are usually mild. But sometimes, heat waves bring higher temperatures. The state's coastline occasionally experiences flooding. That can happen after a hurricane strikes.

Further Evidence

Look at the website below. Does it give any new evidence to support Chapter One?

Connecticut

abdocorelibrary.com/discovering-connecticut

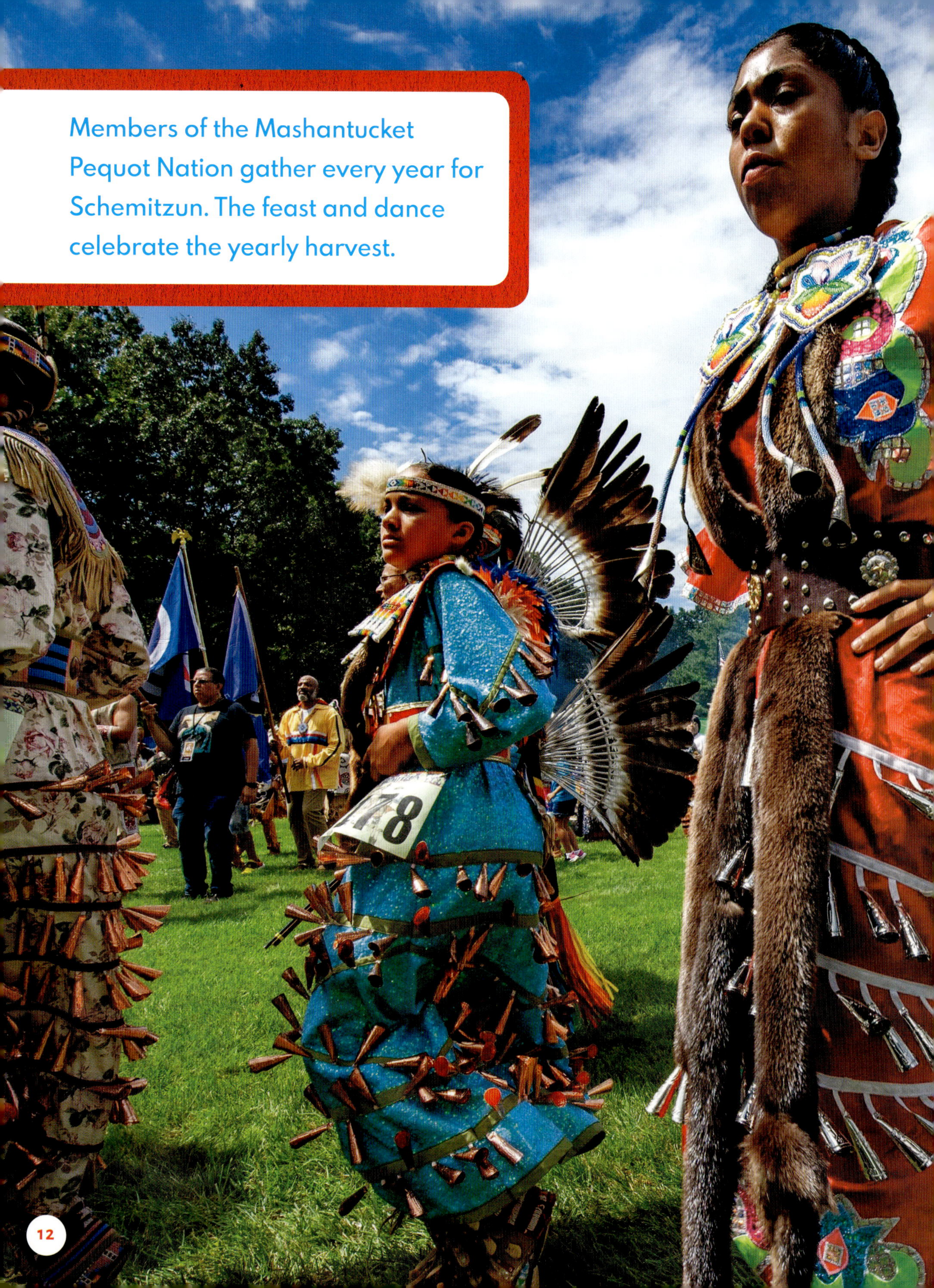

Members of the Mashantucket Pequot Nation gather every year for Schemitzun. The feast and dance celebrate the yearly harvest.

CHAPTER 2

The People of Connecticut

The first people in Connecticut came around 10,000 years ago. They hunted and gathered their food. They also used stone tools. American Indian peoples such as the Pequot and Mohegan later grew crops. These included corn, beans, and squash.

Today, Connecticut recognizes five American Indian nations. These are the Eastern Pequot, the Mashantucket Pequot, the Mohegan, the Schaghticoke, and the Golden Hill Paugussett. Today, around 0.7 percent of people in Connecticut are American Indians.

Dutch and English settlers arrived in Connecticut starting in 1614. They colonized the land and traded with the local American Indians. Many **immigrants** arrived in Connecticut in the 1800s. They came from Ireland, Italy, Poland, French Canada, Russia, and other countries. Black people came to the Northeast from the South in the 1900s. Today, 64 percent of the state's population is white. About 18 percent of people are Hispanic

Early Dutch traders sailed up the Connecticut River to what is now Hartford. At that time, the city was called Fort Good Hope.

or Latino. Black people make up 13 percent of Connecticut's population. Asian people make up 5 percent.

The men's and women's basketball teams at the University of Connecticut play their home games at Gampel Pavilion.

Culture

Lobsters, clams, and oysters are popular in Connecticut. People in the state also have a special way of preparing their burgers. Instead of cooking the burgers on a stove or grill, people steam them. This makes the burgers extra juicy.

There are a lot of college basketball fans in Connecticut. The men's and women's basketball teams at the University of Connecticut often draw large crowds. Home games can have more than 10,000 people in the stands.

Big Name in Basketball

Both the men's and women's basketball teams at the University of Connecticut have been very successful. The men's team has won five national championships. The women's team has won 11. The teams have won titles in the same year twice. They did it in 2004 and again in 2014.

More than 200,000 bushels of oysters are harvested in Connecticut every year.

Industry

Connecticut has a large **manufacturing** industry. Many people create transportation equipment. Others work in electronics or machinery.

Other people sell **insurance** and land. Some people raise oysters. They sell the oyster meat.

Each year, Connecticut oysters are eaten at the Norwalk Oyster Festival. Harry Rilling, the mayor of Norwalk, talked about the town's festival:

> Every year we get thousands of visitors, many from across the state, who come to enjoy incredible food, including local grown oysters.

Source: R. J. Scofield. "Norwalk Oyster Festival Promises Weekend of Fun for Everyone." *Patch*, 7 Sept. 2023, patch.com. Accessed 8 Sept. 2023.

What's the Big Idea?

Read this quote carefully. What is its main idea? Explain how the main idea is supported by details.

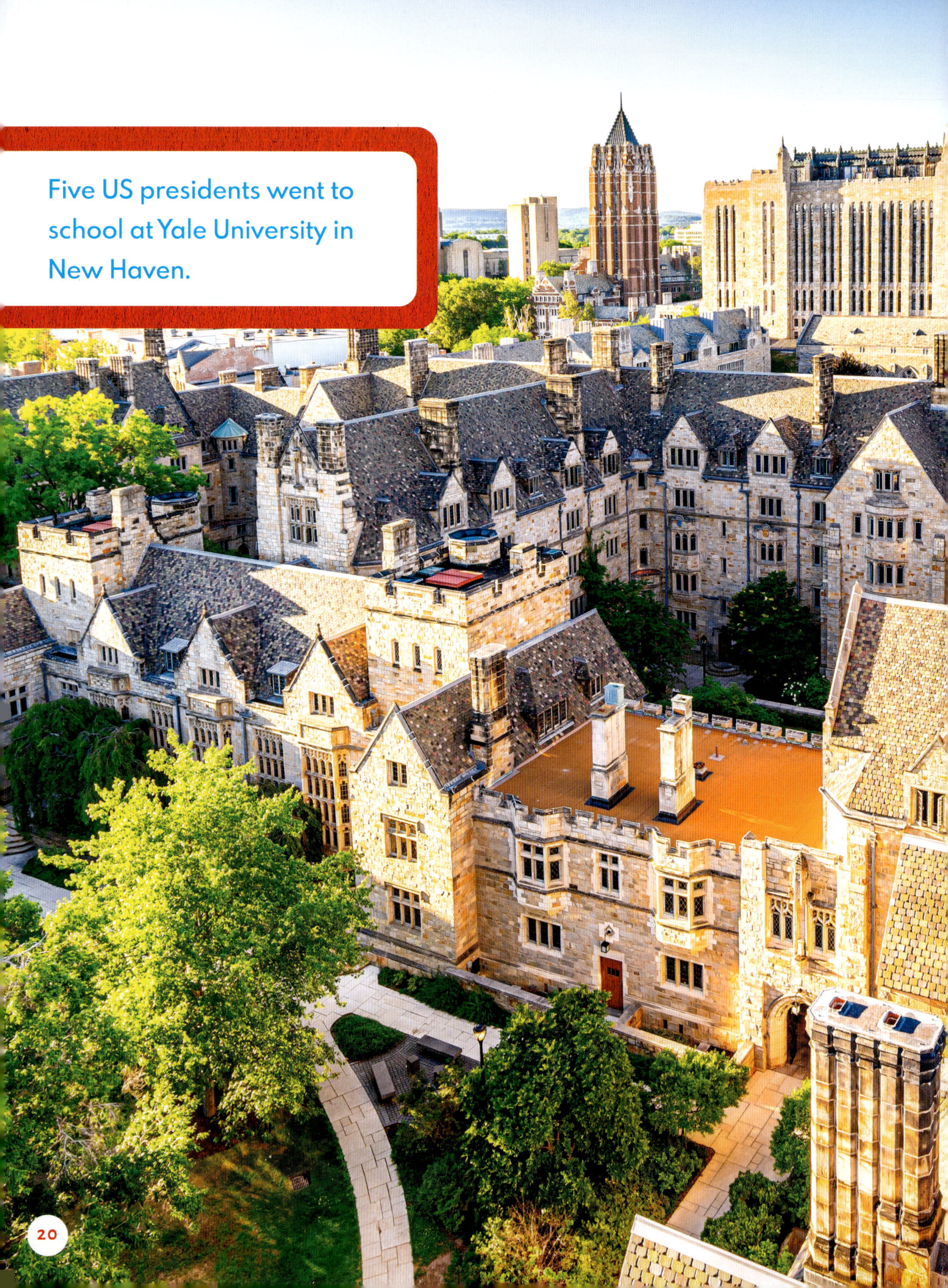

Five US presidents went to school at Yale University in New Haven.

CHAPTER 3

Places in Connecticut

The largest city in Connecticut is Bridgeport. At the city's Beardsley Zoo, visitors can see many animals, including alligators, leopards, and wolves. Hartford is the capital city. Other large cities include New Haven and Stamford.

Much of the Gillette Castle was built from local Connecticut stones.

New Haven is home to Yale University. It is one of the oldest universities in the United States.

Parks and Nature

Gillette Castle State Park in East Haddam is named after a castle in the park. But no royalty ever lived in this castle. It was actually built by actor William Hooker Gillette in the early 1900s. The castle was his home before the land it is on became a state park. Visitors can tour the inside of the castle. They can also camp nearby.

Hammonasset Beach State Park is in Madison, Connecticut. It is the state's largest beach park. Visitors can relax in the sand or swim in the Atlantic Ocean.

The *Charles W. Morgan* is the last wooden whaling ship in the world that still floats.

Every year, hikers pass through the state on the Appalachian Trail. The trail is 2,198 miles (3,537 km) long. One end is in Maine. The other is in Georgia. It passes through 14 eastern states, including Connecticut.

Landmarks

Although Connecticut is one of the smallest states, it is full of interesting landmarks. The Mystic Seaport is one of Connecticut's most popular places for tourists. It has many old boats floating in its water. One of them is the *Charles W. Morgan*. It is an old **whaling** ship.

Mark Twain House and Museum

Mark Twain is a famous American author. He wrote many books during the late 1800s. In 1871, he and his family moved to Hartford. They eventually built a house there. Many of Mark Twain's most popular works were written in that house. Today, people can visit the Mark Twain House and Museum.

The Boulder Dash ride at Lake Compounce ranks as one of the best wooden roller coasters in the world.

People can learn about the 37 whaling **voyages** it took in the 1800s and early 1900s.

Visitors seeking excitement can find it at Lake Compounce, near Bristol. It is the oldest operating amusement park in the United States.

The park opened in 1846 in Bristol. It has many kinds of rides for people of all ages. There are also waterslides and pools.

Connecticut has something for everyone. Visitors can enjoy its parks and beaches. They can taste its delicious seafood dishes. And they can study its important role in US history as one of the 13 original colonies.

Explore Online

Visit the website below. What new information did you learn about Mystic Seaport that wasn't in Chapter Three?

Mystic Seaport Museum

abdocorelibrary.com/discovering-connecticut

State Map

KEY

Capital

Park

City or town

Point of interest

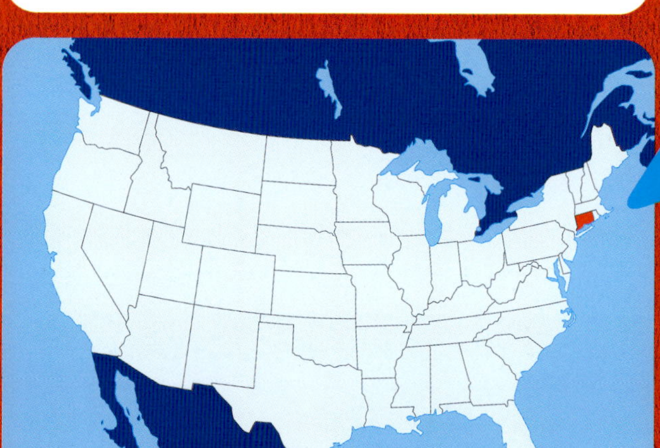

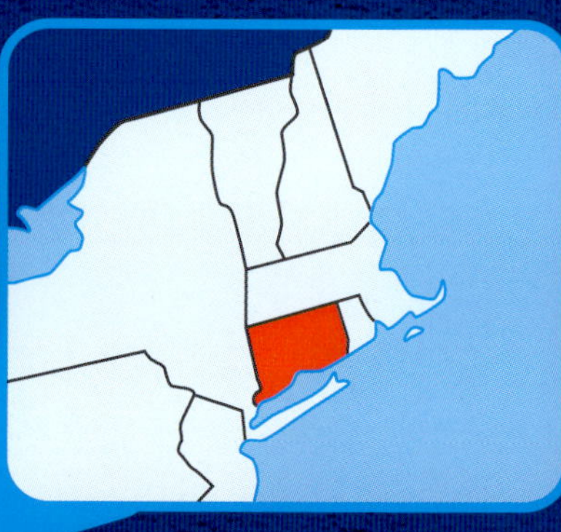

Kent Falls State Park

Yale University

Connecticut: The Constitution State

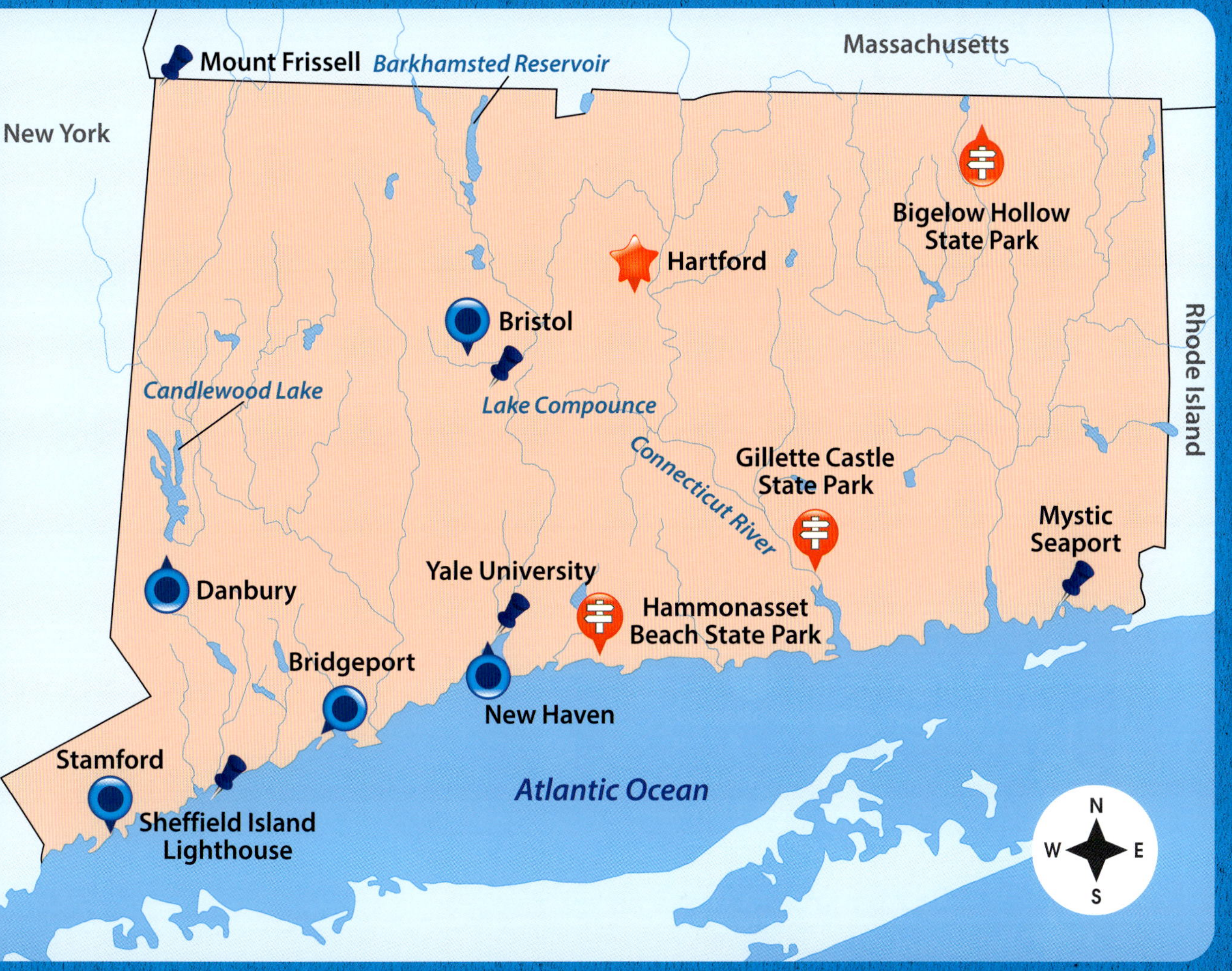

Glossary

colonies
areas that are controlled by another country

colonists
people who have moved to and taken control of an area

immigrants
people who move to a different country

insurance
a legal agreement where a person gets financial protection in an emergency situation

manufacturing
the process of making goods to sell

provisions
supplies such as food and equipment

voyages
long journeys at sea

whaling
the practice of hunting whales

Online Resources

To learn more about Connecticut, visit our free resource websites below.

Visit **abdocorelibrary.com** or scan this QR code for free Common Core resources for teachers and students, including vetted activities, multimedia, and booklinks, for deeper subject comprehension.

Visit **abdobooklinks.com** or scan this QR code for free additional online weblinks for further learning. These links are routinely monitored and updated to provide the most current information available.

Learn More

Kavon, Kana. *The 50 States: Amazing Landscapes, Fascinating People, Wonderful Wildlife*. DK, 2021.

Tieck, Sarah. *Connecticut*. Abdo, 2020.

Index

About the Author

Ib Larsen is a writer and an editorial assistant living in Saint Paul, Minnesota.